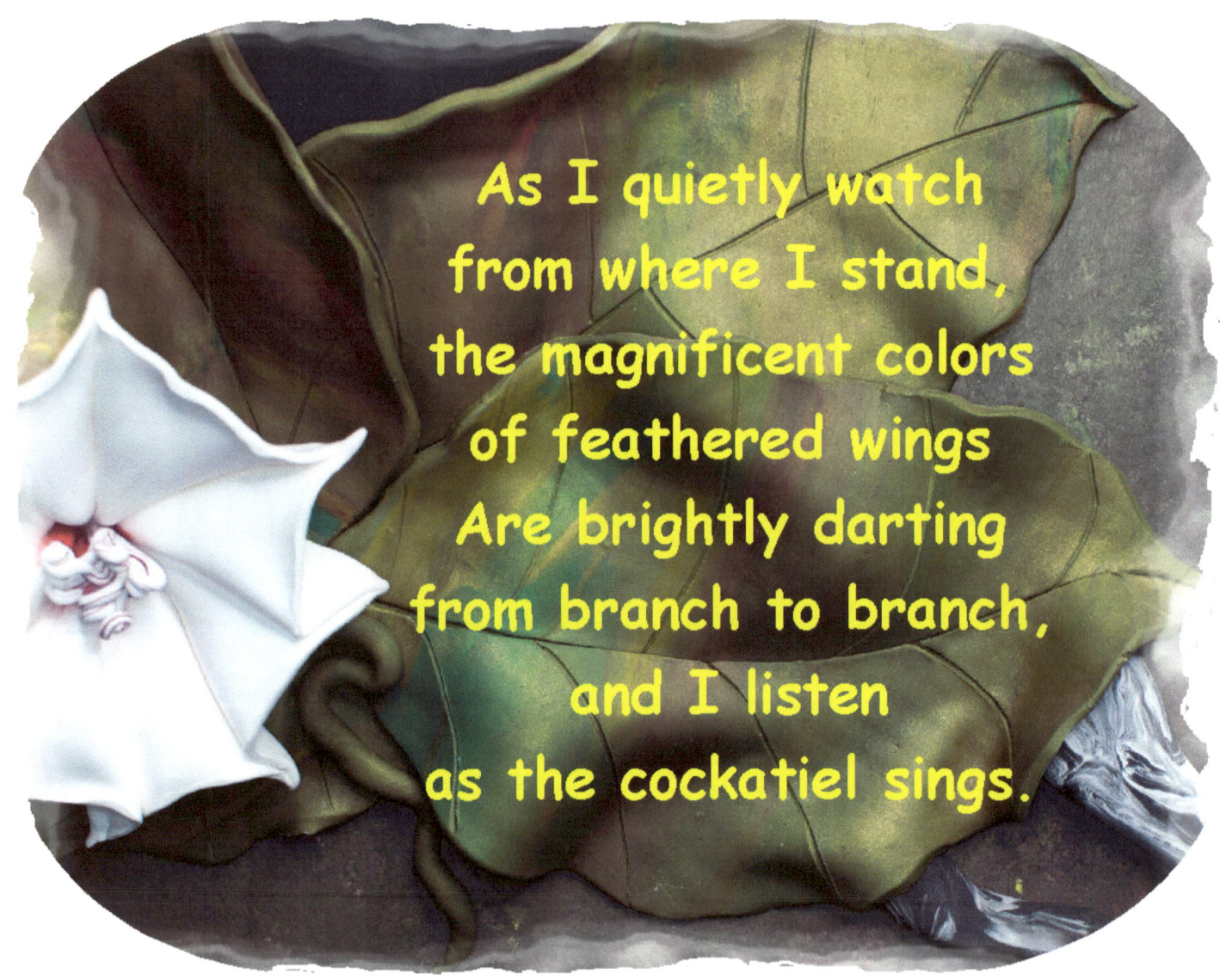

As I quietly watch
from where I stand,
the magnificent colors
of feathered wings
Are brightly darting
from branch to branch,
and I listen
as the cockatiel sings.

4

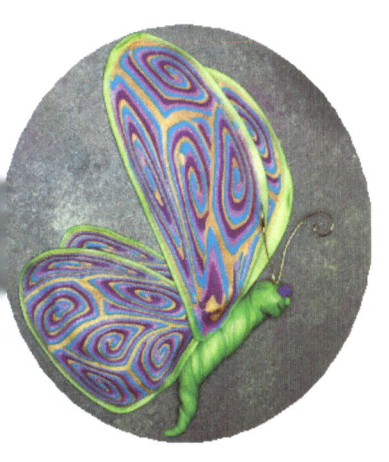

Acknowledgements:

Special thanks to my granddaughter, Rachael, for keeping the child within me alive and filled with wonderful imagination.

Thank you to Shane Marshall for his expertise in editing and his photography of my artwork.

www.shanemarshallphotos.weebly.com

The illustrations for this book were created in polymer clay by the author, Rhonda Peters

www.laffingart.com ~ 517-398-1340

In the recesses of my
imaginary rainforest,
deep within the lovely
leaves and flowers,
Live the creatures
hiding there,
and in my mind
they play for hours.

2

And the toucan boldly
tells his tale,
as he chatters from
his perch on high.
Even the
smallest creatures,
among the curly fronds,
hear his boisterous cry.

6

The twining vines
climb up the trees,
and wind their way back
down again,
Creating pathways
to the sun,
up and out of
the forest dim.

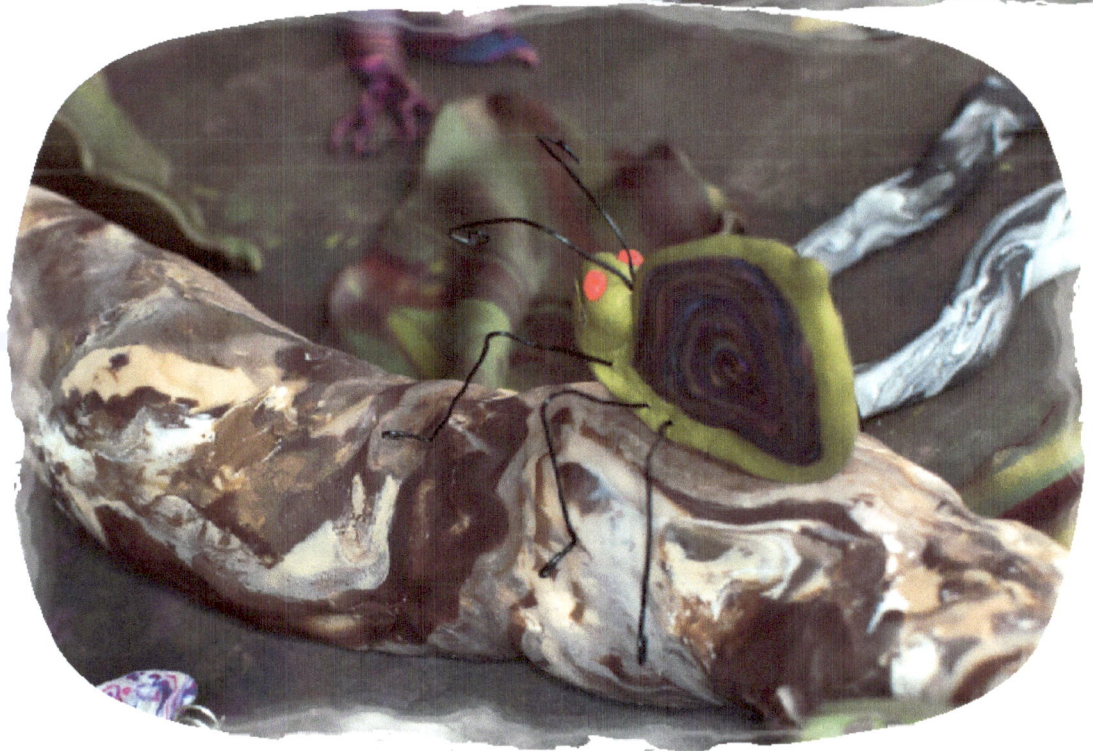

What are the birds
so excited about?
Who are they chattering
to below?
The monkey seeks
the shelter of the leaves,
to secretly watch this
wondrous show.

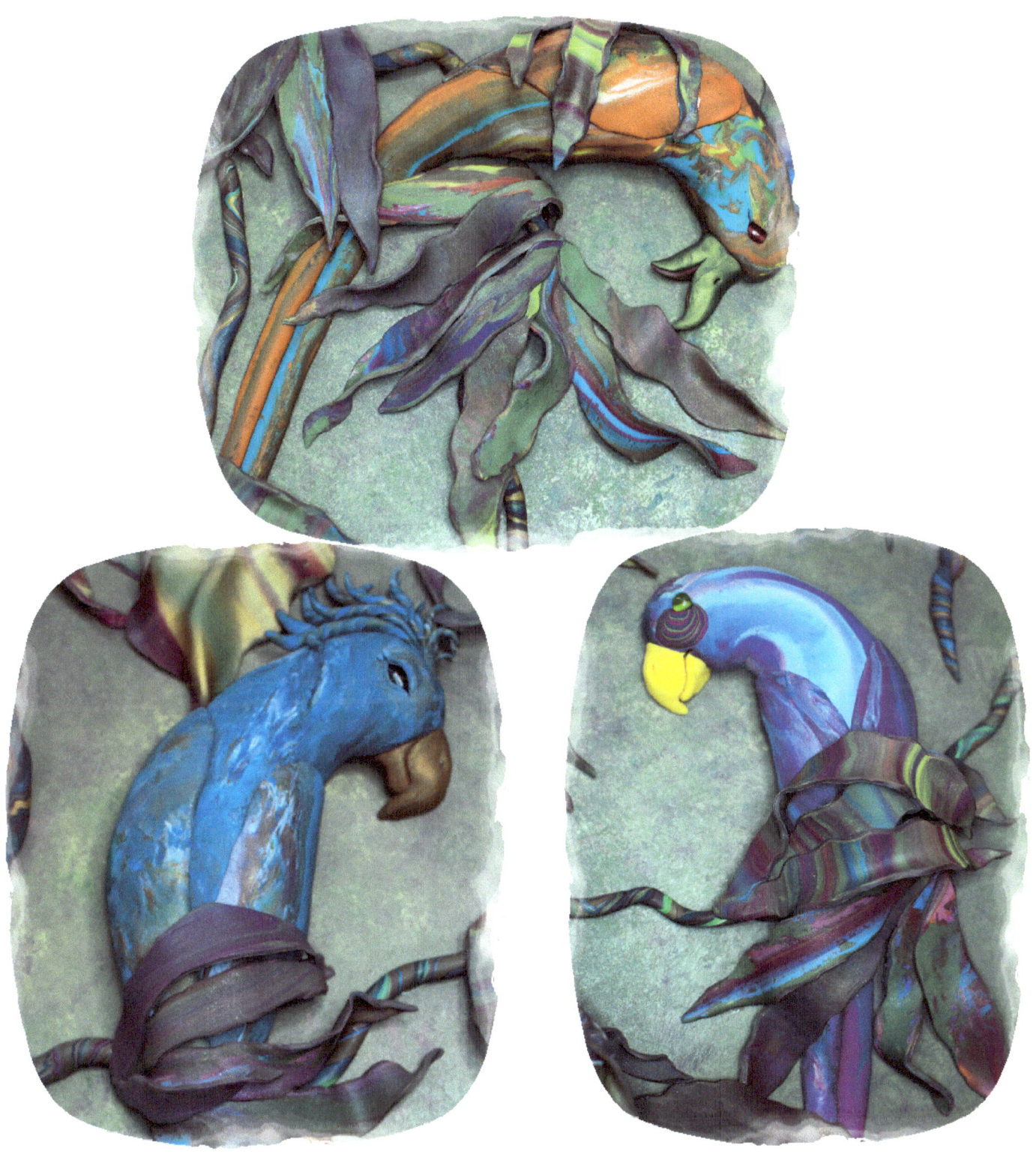

I hear him chuckle
as a curious butterfly
flutters closely at the
corner of my eye,
Sipping sweet nectar
from extraordinary blooms,
in secret silence
flying by.

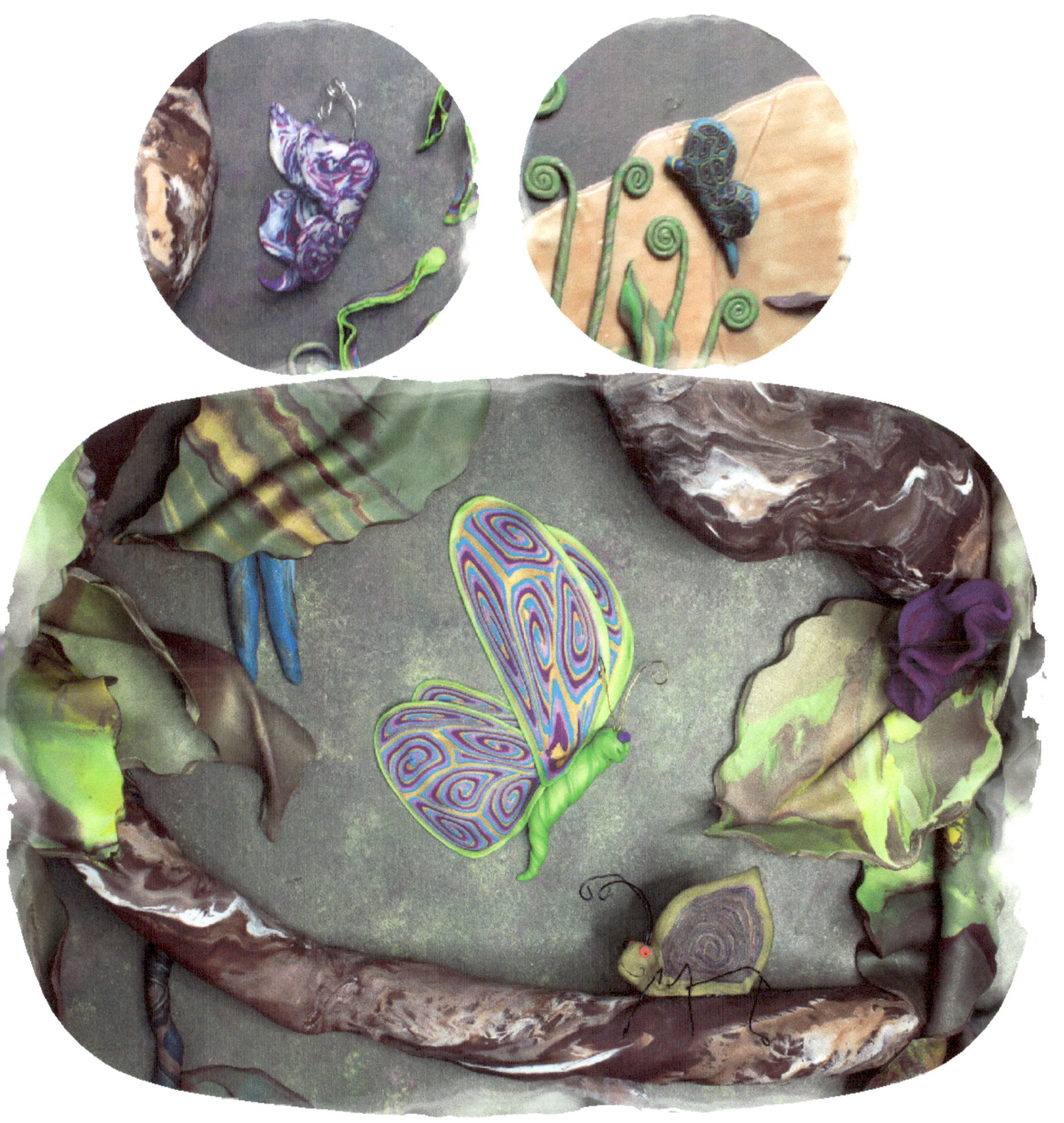

The kaleidoscope frog
in brilliant color,
looks upon a feast
fit for a king.
Croaking,
"Galunk, galunk,"
for his supper
he does sing.

14

There sits in quiet,
peaceful splendor,
watching from
a tigerwood branch,
In a reflection of
its surrounding colors,
the chameleon,
changing at every chance.

16

The crinkly-beaked hummer
in colorful attire,
buzzes along from
flower to flower,
Busily slurping up
lots of sweet syrup,
dashing and soaring
with replenished power.

Up high on a vine
the toady sits,
soaking up
the sun's bright light.
Glowing softly
by end of day,
one little toady
lights up the night.

The little fireflies
come out to play,
blinking and darting
from here to there,
The day is growing
ever short,
And still the monkey
will not share!

22

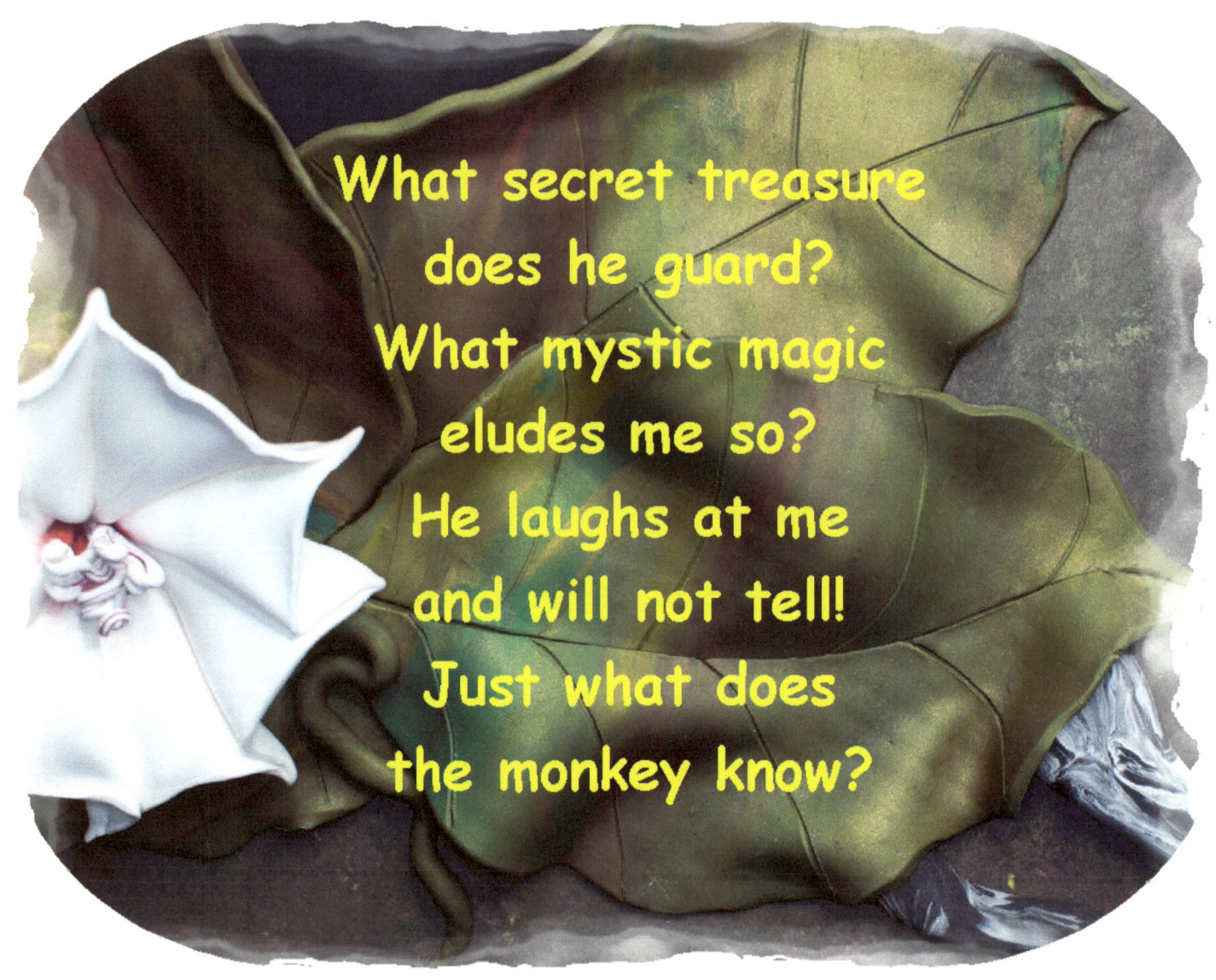

What secret treasure
does he guard?
What mystic magic
eludes me so?
He laughs at me
and will not tell!
Just what does
the monkey know?

24

What Does The Monkey Know? was created by author and polymer clay artist, Rhonda Peters.

The original artwork was created in sections from polymer clay and mounted onto a wood panel. It was entered into competition at ArtPrize in Grand Rapids, MI in 2012 and then became the focal point for this book. As each section was completed Rhonda wrote a new verse to the poem describing the scene as she saw it from her mind's eye.

What Does The Monkey Know? resides at Gallery 49 in Reading, MI, as well as, many other pieces created by Rhonda. To learn more about the work Rhonda does please visit her website, www.laffingart.com.

Protect Our Rain Forests.
10% of your purchase of
"What Does The Monkey Know?"
will be donated to the
Rainforest Foundation
to help prevent the
destruction of
rainforests worldwide.
Thank you!